Earthworms

By Megan Borgert-Spaniol

BELLWETHER MEDIA · MINNEAPOLIS, MN

Note to Librarians, Teachers, and Parents:

Blastoff! Readers are carefully developed by literacy experts and combine standards-based content with developmentally appropriate text.

Level 1 provides the most support through repetition of high-frequency words, light text, predictable sentence patterns, and strong visual support.

Level 2 offers early readers a bit more challenge through varied simple sentences, increased text load, and less repetition of high-frequency words.

Level 3 advances early-fluent readers toward fluency through increased text and concept load, less reliance on visuals, longer sentences, and more literary language.

Level 4 builds reading stamina by providing more text per page, increased use of punctuation, greater variation in sentence patterns, and increasingly challenging vocabulary.

Level 5 encourages children to move from "learning to read" to "reading to learn" by providing even more text, varied writing styles, and less familiar topics.

Whichever book is right for your reader, Blastoff! Readers are the perfect books to build confidence and encourage a love of reading that will last a lifetime!

This edition first published in 2014 by Bellwether Media, Inc.

No part of this publication may be reproduced in whole or in part without written permission of the publisher. For information regarding permission, write to Bellwether Media, Inc., Attention: Permissions Department, 5357 Penn Avenue South, Minneapolis, MN 55419.

Library of Congress Cataloging-in-Publication Data

Borgert-Spaniol, Megan, 1989-
  Earthworms / by Megan Borgert-Spaniol.
    pages cm. – (Blastoff! readers. Backyard wildlife)
  Audience: Grades K to 3.
  Includes bibliographical references and index.
  Summary: "Developed by literacy experts for students in kindergarten through grade three, this book introduces earthworms to young readers through leveled text and related photos"– Provided by publisher.
  ISBN 978-1-60014-919-1 (hardcover : alk. paper)
  1. Earthworms–Juvenile literature. I. Title.
  QL391.A6B67 2014
  592'.64–dc23
                                                                      2013000903

Printed in the United States of America, North Mankato, MN.

Contents

Earthworms are long, soft animals. Their bodies have many **segments**.

segments

Earthworms are covered in small hairs. The hairs help them move.

hairs

Earthworms are found in forests, grasslands, and gardens. They live in **soil**.

They stay in the **damp** soil during the day. Their bodies would dry up in the sun.

Earthworms come to the surface at night. They also appear when it rains.

Sometimes danger waits at the surface. Earthworms are **prey** for birds, snakes, and other **predators**.

Earthworms search for food at the surface. They bring bits of plants into their **burrows**.

Earthworms also eat soil as they move underground. Their tunnels help the soil hold water.

Earthworms
bring healthy soil
to the surface.
This helps new
plants grow!

Glossary

burrows—holes or tunnels that some animals dig in the ground

damp—slightly wet

predators—animals that hunt other animals for food

prey—animals that are hunted by other animals for food

segments—parts that connect; an earthworm's segments look like rings.

soil—the earth in which plants grow

To Learn More

AT THE LIBRARY

Himmelman, John. *An Earthworm's Life*. New York, N.Y.: Children's Press, 2000.

Kalman, Bobbie. *The Life Cycle of an Earthworm*. New York, N.Y.: Crabtree Pub., 2004.

Pfeffer, Wendy. *Wiggling Worms at Work*. New York, N.Y.: HarperCollins, 2004.

ON THE WEB

Learning more about earthworms is as easy as 1, 2, 3.

1. Go to www.factsurfer.com.

2. Enter "earthworms" into the search box.

3. Click the "Surf" button and you will see a list of related Web sites.

With factsurfer.com, finding more information is just a click away.

Index

The images in this book are reproduced through the courtesy of: Antagain, front cover; Minden Pictures/ Masterfile, p. 5; Philippe Clement/ Nature Picture Library, pp. 7, 11; Nomad/ Superstock, p. 7 (small); Vinicius Tupinamba, p. 9; Konzeptm, p. 9 (left); Juan Martinez, pp. 9 (middle), 15 (right); Larisa Lofitskaya, p. 9 (right); Zelijko Radojko, p. 13; Andrew Bailey/ FLPA/ Age Fotostock, p. 15; David Carillet, p. 15 (left); H Schmidbauer/ Age Fotostock, p. 17; Minden Pictures/ SuperStock, p. 19; Maryna Pleshkun, p. 21; Sergii Figurnyi, p. 21 (plant).